The Mind's Eye

Using pictures creatively in language learning

Alan Maley, Alan Duff and Françoise Grellet

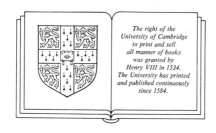

The right of the
University of Cambridge
to print and sell
all manner of books
was granted by
Henry VIII in 1534.
The University has printed
and published continuously
since 1584.

Cambridge University Press

Cambridge

London   New York   New Rochelle

Melbourne   Sydney

Published by the Press Syndicate of the University of Cambridge
The Pitt Building, Trumpington Street, Cambridge CB2 1RP
32 East 57th Street, New York, NY 10022, USA
10 Stamford Road, Oakleigh, Melbourne 3166, Australia

© Cambridge University Press 1980

First published 1980
Fourth printing 1986

Printed in Hong Kong by
Wing King Tong Company Ltd

ISBN 0 521 23332 1 Student's Book
ISBN 0 521 23333 X Teacher's Book

KY

Contents

Acknowledgements

The authors and publishers are grateful to those listed below for permission to reproduce illustrations. It has not been possible to identify the sources of all the illustrations used and in such cases the publishers would welcome information from copyright owners. The numbers refer to the illustrations.

Photographs
Dominic Sansoni (1.2, 2.7, 3.6, 4.4, 4.6, 5.1, 7.3, 14.1); Jason Strevens (1.6, 5.2, 5.5, 8.2, 8.6); Central Office of Information (1.3); Petros Gondicas (1.7, 2.4, 14.11, 14.13); George A. Tice (2.1); B. A. King (2.5, 2.6, 6.1); John Hillelson Agency Ltd: photograph by the late Tony Ray-Jones (3.1); John Walmsley (3.2, 14.14); Martin Shallcross (3.3, 4.1, 7.2, 14.2, 14.3); Bob Watkins (3.5, 3.7, 4.2, 7.6, 7.7); Paul Hill (5.7); Times Newspapers Ltd: advertisement (6.3), photographs from *The Sunday Times* (6.4, 14.15); Jeanloup Sieff (6.7); Camera Press Ltd (7.4); Rex Features Ltd (7.5); William Collins & Sons Co. Ltd: photograph from *The End of the Game* by Peter Beard (8.7); Manpower Services Commission (14.16); Bruno Bischofsberger (14.17); Weidenfeld & Nicolson Ltd: photograph by Ronald C. James from *The Intelligent Eye* by R. L. Gregory (15.2).
Photographs by Françoise Grellet: 1.1, 1.5, 2.3, 3.4, 4.3, 4.7, 5.3, 5.4, 5.6, 7.1, 14.4–14.10.
Photographs by Alan Duff: 1.4, 4.5, 5.7, 6.2, 8.1, 8.3, 11.1, 11.2.

Paintings and drawings
Richard S. Zeisler & Co: *Les Amants* by René Magritte (10.1); Museum of Modern Art, New York: *L'Empire des Lumières, II, Le Faux Miroir* by René Magritte (10.2, 10.8 and front cover); National Gallery of Victoria: *L'Eloge de la Dialectique* (10.4); Museum Boymans-van Beuningen, Rotterdam: *La Reproduction Interdite* by René Magritte (10.5); all paintings by René Magritte © ADAGP, Paris 1979; Escher Foundation, Haags Gemeentemuseum, The Hague: *Eye, Relativity, Dew Drop* by M. C. Escher (10.3, 10.9, 10.10); Faith Shannon: detail from bookbinding for *The Genus Crocus* by George Maw, photograph by Tony Evans, (10.6); Georges Fall: *Sanctuaire* by Jiri Kolar (10.7); cartoon by Werner Finck (11.3); Christiane Charillon: drawings by Sempé (11.4, 11.5, 12.1, 13.2, 13.3); Hope, Leresche & Sayle: drawings by Ronald Searle (12.2, 12.3); Editions Jacques Glénat: drawings by Serre (12.4, 12.5, 12.6, 12.7).

Book design by Peter Ducker MSTD

1 Portraits

1.1

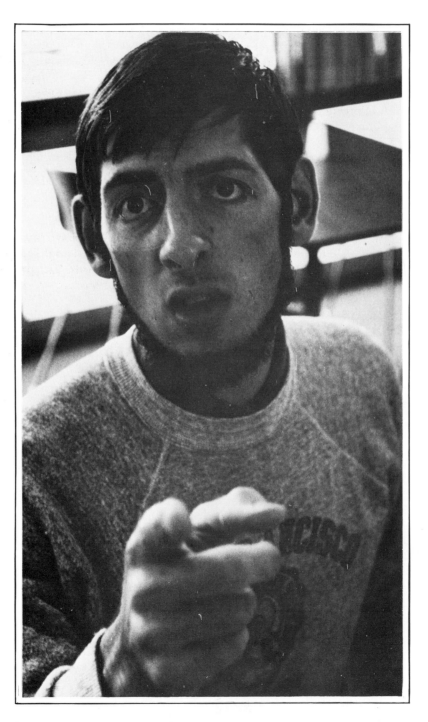

1 Working alone, study the picture opposite for not more than one minute. Then close your eyes, and try to recall the face as exactly as possible. Now, open your eyes and look at the portrait again. Note down your ideas about the following:
   – the young man's age.
   – the language he is speaking (his own, or a foreign language); his manner of speaking (hesitant, fiery, calm, etc.).
   – his mood or emotion at this moment.
2 Compare notes with a partner. Look at the picture in detail together and consider the following:
   – His finger is raised. How do you interpret the gesture? Is he angry, frightened, explaining . . .?
   – His mouth is open. Is he necessarily speaking?
   – Do his eyes suggest how many people are in front of him?
3 Bearing in mind all that you have decided about this young man, write down a fragment (no longer than fifteen words) of what he is saying. Try to suggest as much as possible about the total situation in these words. Each pair reads its fragment aloud; the others listen and draw conclusions from what they hear.

1.2

Work on your own first. Then compare what you've done with your partner(s).
1 Is this young man looking directly at anyone or anything? Does his expression tell you what he is feeling? (Try covering the background with your hand in order to concentrate on his face.) Has he just been moving? Is he likely to move soon?
2 Now compare him with the others in the background. Is he in any way different? (Clothes? Expression?) Does he 'belong' here? Where is he? What is he doing here?
3 If this was a picture at a photography exhibition, what title would you give it?
   If it was an illustration to an article, what would be the title of the article?
   If it was a poster, what would be the text on the poster?

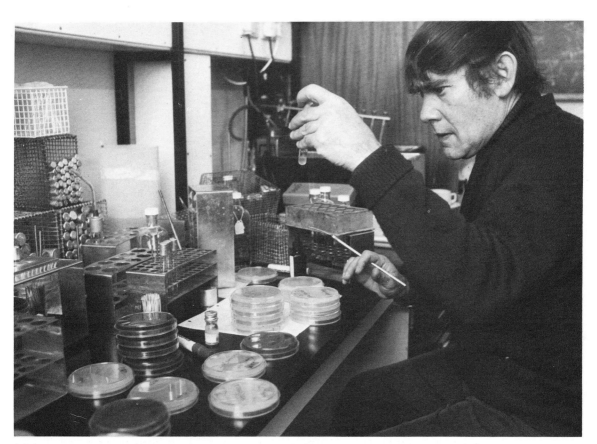

1.3

Work on your own first. Then compare what you've done with your partner(s).

1 *The man*

What is his attitude to the work he is doing? Is he bored, absorbed, excited, worried . . .?

Do you think he is doing his regular job? If not, why not?

Is he wearing the 'right' clothes for this work?

2 *The setting*

Look carefully at the objects in the picture. Try to be as specific as you can in describing where the photo was taken.

Is there anything that seems out of place?

3 If this was a sequence from a film, what kind of film would it be (e.g. science fiction, documentary, adventure)? Write a brief outline of the plot.

1.4

1.5

1 Working on your own, look at either of these portraits, or at the ones on the next page. You are to *become* the person you select. First, 'build up' your personality. You will need to decide:
   – how old you are.
   – what your nationality is.
   – where you were born.
   – what your profession is, etc. (Don't forget to give yourself a name!)
   Concentrate on the details that strike you in the picture, e.g. Are you smoking? Do you wear glasses? Have you got a moustache?

2 Working in groups, each person should choose a portrait from anywhere in the book and become that person. Imagine that he or she is a famous person. Each member of the group will interview and be interviewed in turn. It is up to the interviewer to find out as much as possible about you and, particularly, *why* you are famous. At the end of the 'interview', you should show the interviewer your portrait.

1.6

1.7

2 Objects

2.1

In small groups, look at the picture opposite for two or three minutes.
Decide on an interpretation. Try to answer the following questions:
– Where does it take place? (What room? What kind of house?)
– What exactly are these objects? What are they used for?
– Are they still in use? (Is it water glistening on the china jug?)
– Describe who uses/used them. When? Why?
– Are there any other objects next to them on the table? (Outside the picture?)
– What else is there in the room?
– Is there anybody there? Doing what? Describe the person(s).
– What particular smell do you associate with the scene?
Choose a secretary to write down the group's interpretation.
Each group tells the others what they have imagined. The rest of the class should ask
them as many questions as possible to get a clear idea of what they have thought of
and of what is 'outside the picture'.

Follow-up work

Working in pairs or in small groups, consider the following points:
1 Imagine and describe similar objects (i.e. with the same function):
   – two centuries earlier.
   – two centuries later.
2 Imagine a funny/dramatic/moving/strange incident linked to that particular jug
   and tell your partner/group the story.
3 Imagine this jug and basin have kept a diary. Write ten lines out of this diary,
   describing the most critical/amusing events of their lives.
   e.g. I was made in . . .
      Today they sent me by ship to . . .
      Mr X has bought me . . .
      On the way to . . . they dropped me and . . .
4 Imagine this picture appeared in a newspaper illustrating an arts column/a report
   on a sensational murder/an article on interior design.
   – What caption would accompany the picture?
   – Write out the first paragraph of the article, keeping in mind that the main
     information is usually summed up there.

2.2

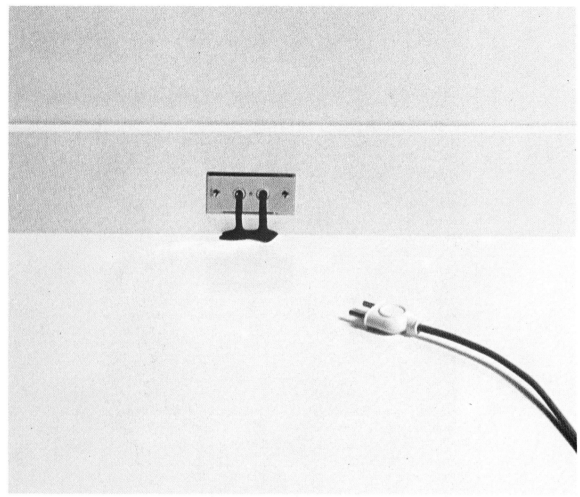

Work on your own first. Then compare what you've done with your partner(s).
1 How do you react to this picture as a whole? Is it a joke?
2 You are about to plug in your tape recorder when you see this. What would you do? Imagine the scene (you might make a telephone call, or have a conversation with someone in the room).
3 Imagine this picture appeared in a newspaper illustrating a sensational murder story or a recent discovery in physics. What would the corresponding headline be?
4 Imagine this picture was part of an advertisement. What was it for? Write out the advertising slogan that accompanied the picture.
5 Working with a partner, choose three or four other pictures from different sections of the book and work out a story linking those pictures with this one. When every pair has found a story, explain what part this particular picture plays in your story.

Work on your own first. Then compare what you've done with your partner(s).
1 Where do you think these dolls are? On a garden fence? Hanging up for sale? Are they stage props? Describe their owners or the people who use them. When are they going to be taken down? What for? What will happen to them next?
2 One of these dolls was yours when you were a child. You are surprised to find it here because you had lost it in a strange way. Describe the incident to your partners.
3 This picture appeared on the cover of a detective story/a love story. What was the title of the book?
4 You found this old photograph in a family album. What was written underneath?
5 Write a short poem about the picture. How does your poem differ from those other people have written?
6 Choose three other objects in this section of the book and combine them all into a story.

2.4

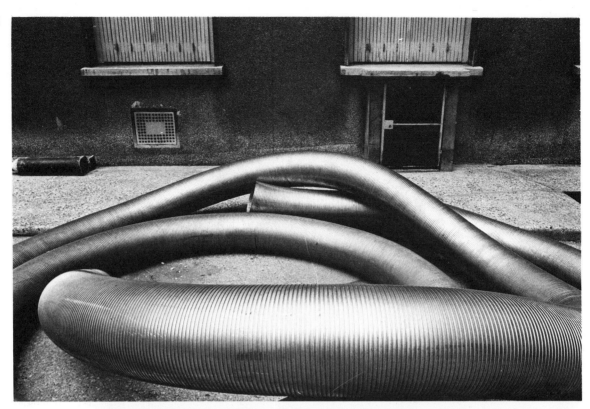

2.5

3 People

3.1

1 Work in pairs and look at the picture opposite for a few minutes. Try to answer the following questions:
  – Where does the scene take place?
  – What is there on the right and left of the picture? Is there a house nearby? What is it like?
  – Who are those two people? Are they husband and wife?
  – Are they on holiday? Is it an ordinary day or a special day?
  – How did they come there? Did they carry the table, chairs and baskets themselves?
  – What time of the day is it? Can you imagine what they did before, and what they will do after they have finished their meal?
  – Why are there so many bags near the lady? Do they just contain food or is there anything else in them?
  – If they were to talk to each other, what would they talk about?
  – Is there anything that worries or interests them at the moment?
  Find a new partner and briefly explain what you think about the picture to him/her.
2 Work in groups of four and look at picture 3.4 on p. 22. Imagine a possible link between the two pictures. Work out your story and explain it to the rest of the class. Other groups will ask questions and point out possible weak points.

Follow-up work

Work on your own first. Then compare what you've done with your partner(s).
1 The lady is looking at a book. What kind of a book do you think it is? Imagine what its title is.
2 This photo is part of a family album. Write out the sentence that appears under it.
3 Imagine someone comes along (e.g. a servant with a telephone message, someone who has lost his way, a tramp). Write out the short dialogue that would ensue.
4 Suppose that, for just thirty seconds, you can share the man's thoughts. Write down what they are.

Work on your own first. Then compare what you've done with your partner(s).

1 Where does the scene take place? In an office? At home? In a school?
2 What is the relationship between the man and the girl?
3 Why is she yawning?
4 Is there anybody else in the same room?
5 Imagine a short dialogue between these two people.
6 This picture appeared in an advertisement. What product was being advertised?
   Write the slogan that accompanied the picture as well as the text underneath (no
   more than five lines).
7 The girl has finished what she was doing and decides to start a letter to a friend,
   telling her about her daily life. Imagine the beginning of her letter.

3.3

Work on your own first. Then compare what you've done with your partner(s).

1 Where are these two men?
2 Who are they? What do they do? What exactly is each of them doing right now? Where are they going?
3 Describe what each of them was doing an hour earlier and will be doing an hour later.
4 Imagine these two men keep a diary. What does each of them write for that day?
5 One of these two men turns round and speaks to the other one. Write out their dialogue.
6 Think of a situation (in their work or in their daily life) in which these two men might meet and speak to each other. What would they say?
7 Look at other pictures in this book and associate each of these two men with:
  – a picture of a woman.
  – an object.
  Justify your choice and compare it with your partner's.
8 Imagine there are two balloons above the heads of these men. In a few lines, write out what thoughts might appear in these balloons.

3.4

3.5

4 Outside

4.1

1 Working in pairs, try first of all to imagine what lies beyond the frame of the picture on the opposite page. Be as precise as possible. Consider these questions:
  – What is the fence made *of* and what was it made *for*? How far does it extend? What lies on this side and what on the other side?
  – Do you think the man is alone? If anyone were to pass, would they be shocked or surprised at what he is doing? Would they think he belonged to the neighbourhood? (i.e. What do his clothes tell us?)
  – Is he looking at something static or something moving? Has he been looking at it for a long time? Is he interested in what he sees? Is he doing anything dangerous or illegal? What will he be doing in five minutes' time?
  Now change partners and discuss your different views of the picture. Change partners again, several times.
2 Now return to your first partner. Look through the book and pick out five other pictures (of which at least two must be from this section) which, taken together with this picture, would make up a story. When your story is ready, find a different partner and try to work out each other's story.

1 Study the picture on your own for about five minutes. Decide as much as you can about the two people.
 – Do you conclude anything about them from the way they are dressed?
 – Have they been speaking to each other, or is the woman just a chance passer-by? Where is she going to?
 – What is the man looking at? Why is the woman holding her hand to her cheek? Is she looking at something or is she thinking?
 – Where is this street? In a small town, a village, a large city? Is it a busy street?
2 Working in pairs, imagine that the woman turns back and speaks to the man. What will she say or ask? How will he reply? Write down this short exchange. Then, assuming that the woman continues on her way, imagine that the next person she meets is the man on the previous page. What will she say to him? Again, note down the exchange. Do the same for another two pictures in this section. Now circulate your 'dialogue-sheets', so that each pair can see what the others have produced.

4.3

1 Working in groups of three, consider this picture carefully. Look for everything
  that will give hints as to who this person might be and what he is doing here. Try
  to find answers to the following questions:
  – Why is the man half-kneeling? Is he just adjusting his luggage?
  – Does the suitcase belong to him? If not, whose is it? Do the other things belong
    to this man?
  – Where is he and why is he there? Is he about to leave or has he just arrived?
  – How did he come? How will he leave?
  – Is he expecting anyone else to come? If so, who?
2 Once you have considered these points, form different groups of three and
  exchange ideas. Then, look for any five pictures in the book which strike you as
  being relevant to this picture. As a group, write out the words you would use to
  link these pictures if they appeared together. (You may decide that they have been
  included in a personal letter, in which case the linking words will be very different
  from those you would use if the pictures appeared in a police dossier.) Once you
  have done this, break up the groups and work in pairs to compare words and
  pictures.

4.4

4.5

4.6

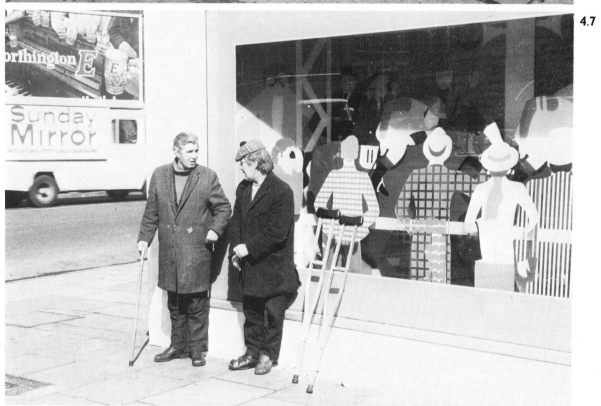

4.7

29

5 Atmosphere

5.1

1 Working in pairs, study the picture opposite for what it *is* rather than what it might be, i.e. let the details speak for themselves. Observe the wallpaper, the window, the table, the chairs, the light switch, wires, decorations, etc.
  – Is this a private home, a café (cheap or expensive?), a hotel, a station buffet?
  – Is anyone else present?
  Look at the woman (her face, her hands, her hair, her clothes). Try to decide who she is, where she is, how long she has been here, how long she will stay, where she is going, what she is thinking about. Note down some of her thoughts.
2 Now change partners. Discuss your different written versions of her thoughts. (Try to speak to at least four other people.) Then return to your first partner and exchange the information you have gathered from others.

Follow-up work

Work on your own first. Then compare what you've done with your partner(s).
1 The woman is in fact waiting for someone. That person never comes. She leaves a note. What does the note say?
2 Later in life, she becomes well-known. In her autobiography, she describes this scene in one short paragraph. Write this paragraph.
3 This is a scene from a film. The woman does not speak, but we hear her thoughts on the soundtrack. Write this part of the soundtrack (the sequence lasts fifty seconds).

1 Working with a partner, find words to fit the picture in the following situations:
   - This photograph was sent to you by an old friend whom you had not seen for a long time. What did he or she write on the back of the picture?
   - This photograph recently appeared on the front pages of several national and international newspapers. It was accompanied by a large headline. What was the headline?
   - This photograph was used on the cover of a best-selling novel. What was the title of the novel?
2 Find four other pictures in this book which could be linked with this one to form a story. Note down your story. Then find a partner and show him or her the pictures you have chosen. Your partner should try to guess your story. (It is important that the details be written so that you do not change your story!)

5.3

1 *Free association*. Do not try to decide what this picture *is*. Allow it, rather, to *suggest* ideas to you. Look at it from different angles, from close up, from far away, upside-down, through a small hole (e.g. through the circle of your thumb and forefinger). Imagine that it is a highly magnified 'blow-up', that it is an aerial photograph, etc. Note down a few words (e.g. hurricane, beach-hut) and compare your impressions with those of your partner. Ask for an explanation if you cannot see what your partner has seen.

2 If this were the cover picture on a record sleeve, what would be the title of the record?

3 If it were a text-book illustration, what chapter would it appear in, or what words would appear beneath it?

4 If it were a picture in an exhibition, what would be the title of the exhibition?

5 If it were classified as 'top-secret', which file would it be placed in and why?

6 Imagine this picture is one of a series of five. Find four other pictures in the book to complete the series.

5.4

5.5

5.6

5.7

35

6 Images

1 Before looking at the picture opposite, write down a single word on a slip of paper. Everyone's words should then be collected. Now the picture can be looked at. The words should be read out slowly. Note down in different columns the words you think *suit* the picture and those you think *conflict* with the picture. Words about which you have no strong feelings should not be noted. Now compare your list with that of others, and discuss points of difference.
2 You can do this in a different way. Look at the picture for only ten seconds. Then look away and write down the first word that comes to mind, no matter how seemingly inappropriate it may be (e.g. elephant, tournament, hardly, etc.).

Follow-up work

In pairs, work as rapidly as possible on the following ideas (time-limits for each idea are given in brackets, but they are only suggestions!).
1 A modern poet (now aged 27) is recalling a scene from his childhood. 'Quote' the five lines of his poem that refer to this moment. (four minutes)
2 A sentence is running through the boy's mind. What is this sentence? (three minutes)
3 Somebody we cannot see is shouting to the boy. What is he or she saying? (two minutes)
4 If you had taken this picture, what title would you give it? (one minute)
5 This picture appeared at an exhibition of photographs on 'Children of the World'. The organiser of the exhibition insisted on putting a quotation or 'wise saying' next to each picture (e.g. 'To see the earth in a grain of sand'). You, the photographer, dislike this. Write a note (not a letter) scribbled on a pad as you left the exhibition, explaining succinctly to the organiser why you did not like the words he put beneath your picture! (The quotations can, of course, be invented.) (five minutes)

Work on your own first. Then compare what you've done with your partner(s).
1 Where are these two objects? On a beach? On a carpet? On a flight of stairs? On a rubbish dump?
2 How did they get there? Is there any connection between them?
3 Are there perhaps other objects nearby which cannot be seen here? If so, what are they?
4 If this was a close-up of two objects that had been left on stage at the end of the first act of a play, what connection would they have had with the action? With a partner, work out the main lines of the action, using any of the portraits on pp. 6–11 as characters in your play. Once your version is ready, exchange it with other pairs.

Work on your own first. Then compare what you've done with your partner(s).
Imagine this picture is one of a series of five pictures all involving a similar macabre
or surrealist technique. In each picture the focus is on a short written message (it
could be a poster, a slogan painted on a wall, a neon sign) against a simple
background.

1 What is this picture an advertisement for? What is the slogan beneath it? Write out
   the slogan.
2 Now make sketches for the four other pictures in this series. The slogan you have
   chosen will, of course, remain the same for each picture, but the words in the
   picture itself will be different.
3 Show a different partner your 'pictures' but not the main slogan. Try to work out
   each other's slogan through questioning based on the sketches.

6.4

6.5

6.6

6.7

41

7 Mystery

7.1

Work in groups of three or four.

Look at the picture opposite for five minutes and clarify all the details it contains.

Work out an explanation of the picture. This will obviously centre upon *who* the man is and *what* he is doing. The following questions might be of help however:

– Where is this taking place? In which country?
– What time of year is it?
– How old is the man?
– Is he real?
– What exactly is he doing?
– Is he alone? Is anyone watching him?
– How long has he been there?
– Is there anything you would expect to see which is not there?
– What has he got on his head?
– Why are his hands in such a peculiar position?

Choose a secretary to write down the group's interpretation.

After ten minutes, the secretary should move to the next group to explain his or her group's interpretation. He or she may be questioned or challenged at this point.

Follow-up work

Work on your own first. Then compare what you've done with your partner(s).

1 A song-writer happened to walk by and observed the man in the photograph. When he got home he wrote a six-line song about what he had seen. Try to write a similar song.

2 This picture appeared in a newspaper to illustrate a practical joke. (That is, a joke to fool the people who saw him.)
 – Find a suitable headline for the article accompanying the picture.
 – Write out the first paragraph of the article, giving all the essential information.

3 The man is on holiday. Write a postcard from him to one of his friends, mentioning the incident in the picture.

Working in pairs or in small groups consider the following points.

1 What is your first reaction to this picture? What do you notice most about it?

2 Imagine you are just behind this person. Suddenly he turns round to ask you something.
   – What do you think he might ask?
   – What would he look like from the front?
   – How would you react?

3 Imagine this picture is on a poster. What do you think is being publicised? What would the slogan be?

4 Imagine you are this person. You are worried. What are some of the things you are worried about?

5 Look carefully at the way this person is dressed and at his hands. Try to imagine the story of his life. Then tell your partner and compare it with his or her version.

6 Choose four other pictures from different sections of the book and link them with this one to form a story. When you have finished tell your story to another pair and get them to tell you theirs.

Working in pairs or in small groups consider the following points.

1 Who do you think this is? What exactly is she doing? Write down your ideas, then exchange them with others.

2 Write down the things you think may be passing through her head.

3 Choose three pictures from the 'Portraits' section (pp. 6–11) of this book. These three people are all involved in a story with this woman. Work out the story with a partner, then tell another pair.

4 Imagine this picture appears in a collection of illustrated poems. It is entitled 'Waiting'. Write the eight-line poem that accompanies it.

5 The woman gets tired of waiting and leaves a note for the person she is waiting for on the window sill behind her. What does the note say? Write it out.

6 You are watching this scene. Suddenly two policemen come up to the woman and arrest her. Why? Work out your explanation with a partner. Then defend it to another pair.

7.4

7.5

46

7.6

Hiding

7.7

8 A different view

8.1

Work in groups of three. Look at the picture opposite carefully for two or three minutes without saying anything. Make notes if you like. Discuss your immediate impressions. One of you should act as secretary and write down all the ideas, however unlikely.

Now come to an agreement about which of the interpretations is the most acceptable or plausible. In order to do so you might consider the following:
– What time of day is it? Is this important?
– Would this scene be the same a few hours later?
– If you were here what would you do?
– What would you expect to see when you reach the top?
– What do you think there is to the left and to the right of the picture?

All groups should come to a decision within a given time. One person in each group should then move to another group. By questioning, the newcomer should attempt to find out what interpretation the others have found and vice versa. Criticism and discussion will follow.

Follow-up work

Work on your own first. Then compare what you've done with your partner(s).
1 You are present. An element of danger is involved. What do you do?
2 You were present. Something happened. You had to send a telegram. Write this telegram quickly (not more than ten words).
3 You read a report of this in the morning paper. What was the headline?
4 Write a poem to describe how you felt when you were in that situation. The poem should not be more than five lines, and no more than three words per line.
   Remember that poems do not necessarily have to rhyme.
5 If you were painting this, what colours would you use?
6 Turn the picture on its side. Does this change your interpretation?

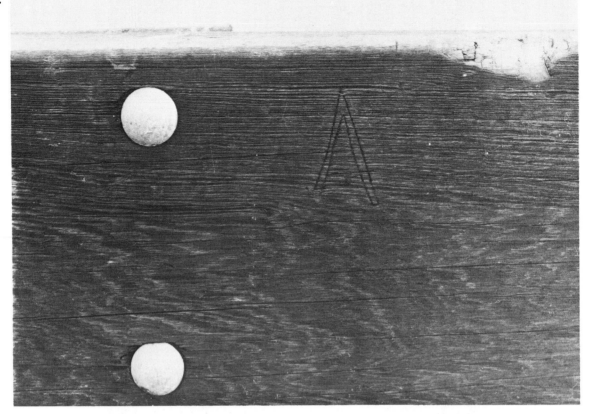

Work on your own first. Then compare what you've done with your partner(s).

1 Study this picture.
   – How far away was it taken?
   – Is it a close-up? Of what?
   – Is it an aerial view? What does it represent?
   – What is it made of?
   – What would it feel like if you touched it?
   – What are the two round things?
   – How can you explain the white line on one side of the picture?

2 There is a sign that looks like a V in the middle of the picture. What is it? Who put it there? What for? Supposing it is an inscription, does it stand for any word(s)? Which one(s)?

3 This inscription is linked to a strange incident that happened to you. Tell your partner about it.

4 Imagine what is around this picture. Is it part of something larger? (A field? Can it be moved?)

5 How were you looking at this picture when deciding on these points? Does it make any difference if you turn it round?

6 Imagine this picture appeared in a geographical magazine. What words would accompany it?

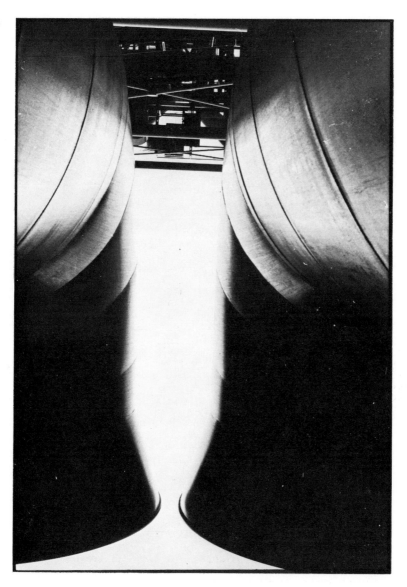

1 Turn this picture round until you think you can make something out of it. What is your main reaction? Do you find it oppressive, threatening, or just technical? Then tell a partner what it suggests.

2 In pairs, study the picture more closely and try to imagine what it could represent. How far away was the photographer? Try to associate the picture with a sound or a smell.

3 Imagine this picture appeared on the cover of a detective story. What would the title be?

4 Find three other pictures (in this book or in magazines) that also seem to represent some abstract design. Look at them with a partner and try to arrange them in a certain order (according to the shapes, the colours, etc.). Then find another partner and show him or her your four pictures in the order you have decided on. Your partner should try to work out why they appear in that particular order.

8.4

8.5

8.6

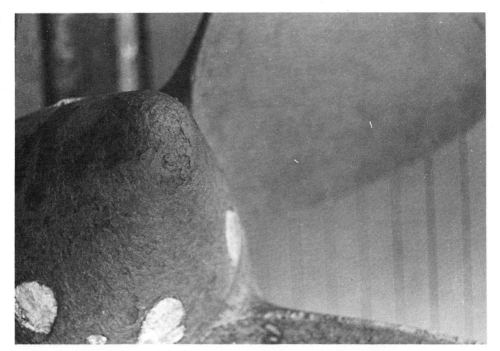

8.7

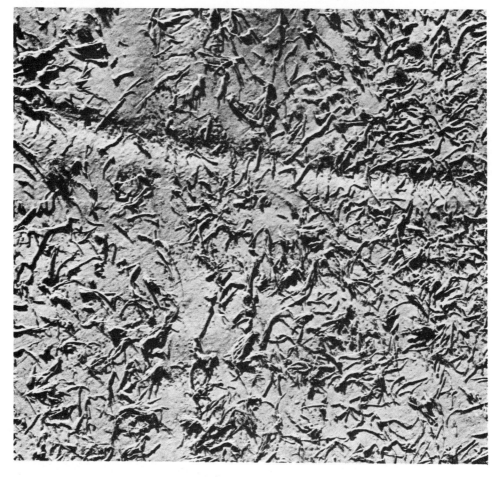

9 Collages

9.1

1 Work in pairs and find connections between any two, three or four of the pictures opposite. Note down your ideas, then change partners and compare notes.
2 Now work in groups of four and try to decide why these pictures were selected and arranged this way. (e.g. Is there a common theme? Have they all been taken from a single picture or series of pictures? Do they have a single purpose?)
3 Working on your own, consider the following list of adjectives:
soothing
exhilarating
irritating
boring
unnerving
frightening
puzzling
annoying
disturbing

Decide which of these adjectives best describe your reaction to the collage. Form groups of three and compare your choices. Add other adjectives if you wish. After explaining why you feel the way you do, try to agree on an order of importance for your group (e.g. 1 puzzling, 2 disturbing, 3 frightening, etc.).

Still in groups of three, try to link the elements in the collage into a story. The adjectives you have just chosen should be the key-note for the story.

Follow-up work

1 Find a title for the collage.
2 Write a four-line poem to illustrate your reaction to the collage. Use at least one of the adjectives listed above.
3 If this collage were to be used for decoration where would you put it? How big would it be?
4 Can you think of any other specific uses for it?
5 What piece of music would go best with this collage?

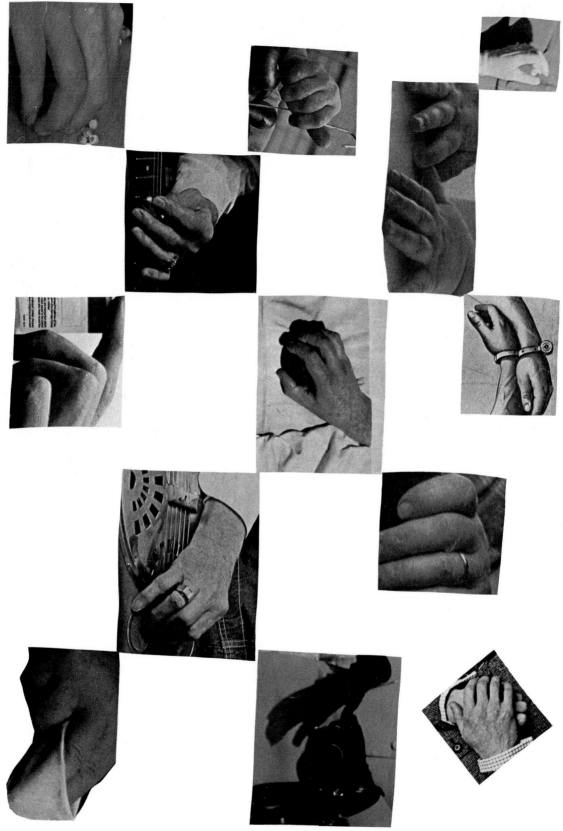

9.3

Work on your own first. Then compare what you've done with your partner(s).

1 Imagine this picture appeared on the cover of a detective story or science-fiction story. What is the title of the book?
2 If you had to give a one-word title to this picture, what would it be?
3 Write a six-line poem to illustrate this picture.
4 If you had to add two shapes or objects, what would they be?
5 Imagine one of the people shown in a picture in this book has just taken off the mask. Which one? Why?
6 Each of the five elements in the picture is involved in a story. Work out the story.

10 Surrealism

10.1

1 Working on your own, look at the picture opposite and consider these questions:
   – Where is this taking place? What is outside the frame of the picture?
   – Is it real or imaginary? (i.e. In a dream? In a film?)
   – Who are the two people? What kind of people are they? What might their jobs be?
   – Why are their heads covered?
   – What are they thinking about?
   – What is your own reaction to the picture? What makes you feel like this?
   – What do you think the painter wanted people to understand?
   Note down your answers.
2 In groups of three exchange answers and discuss them. Find your own title for the picture.

Follow-up work

Work in pairs or small groups.
1 Write a short poem to accompany the picture.
2 Describe an incident you have experienced ('live', through reading a story or seeing a film) which was called to mind by this picture.
3 Imagine that this is the sleeve of a pop record. Work out a title.

(Collection, The Museum of Modern Art, New York)

1 Write out in note form your answers to these questions:
  – Where exactly is this? (Which country? Which town or village?)
  – What time of day is it?
  – Who does the house belong to? What kind of person is he or she?
  – What is going on in the upstairs room?
  – How does the picture make you feel?
  Now work with a partner and discuss your answers.
2 Work with a partner and choose three or four other pictures from different sections
  of the book and find a story to link them together. When you have a story
  exchange it with another pair.
3 The scene in the picture is calm. Imagine something happening which might
  disturb this calm (e.g. a speedboat roaring up and stopping in front of the house).
  Write your idea down. Now form groups of four and discuss the ideas. Choose the
  best idea and try to develop a story from it. One person will need to keep notes.
4 Imagine this appeared in the 'Property for sale' columns of a newspaper. In groups
  of three write out the advertisement which accompanied it.

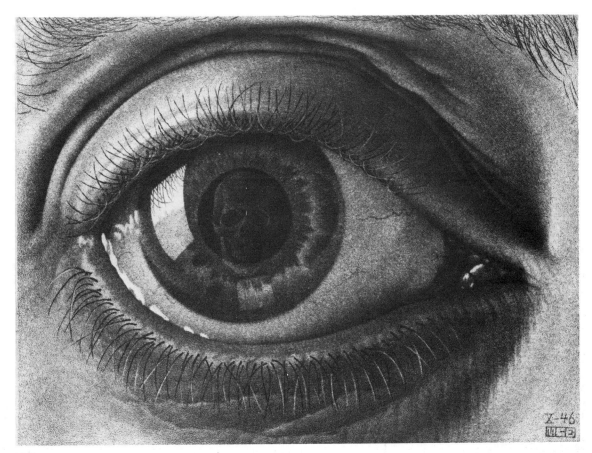

10.3

1 How do you feel when you look at this picture? Try to explain your feelings to a partner.
2 Is the person looking out, or are we looking in? What did the artist 'mean' by the picture? Discuss this with two other people.
3 If this was the cover of a detective novel, what would the title be?
4 If it was a poster in an optician's, what do you think the slogan might be?
5 Work with a partner. One of you should look at the cover of this book (or at any of the pictures of eyes on pp. 64 and 65), the other at this picture. Take turns at describing your picture, so that you have a clear idea of what the differences between your two pictures are.
6 Imagine that this picture formed part of a very vivid dream. What was the rest of the dream? Write it out and exchange dreams with a partner.

10.4

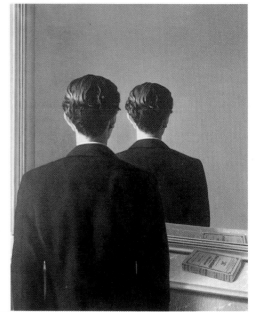

10.5

10.6

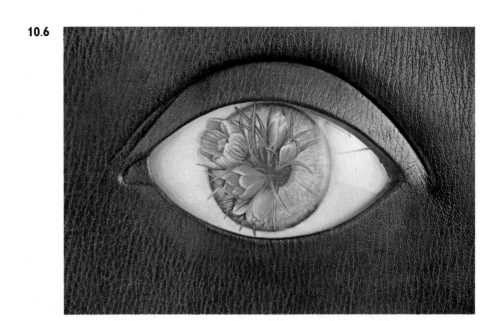

10.7

10.8

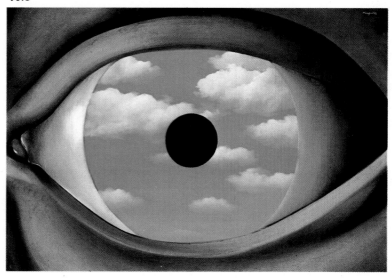

Working in pairs or in small groups, look at the pictures of eyes on pp. 64 and 65 and consider the following points.

1 Which of these adjectives would you associate with each of the three eyes?

sinister	savage
sexy	warm
intriguing	sleepy
piercing	menacing
dreamy	cold

If there are any adjectives which you think fit them better, add them to the list.

2 Imagine they are all advertising something. Which product would you associate with each of them?

If you were advertising the following products, which of the three eyes would you choose for:

a sports car
a perfume for men
a washing powder
a refrigerator
a vacuum cleaner
an air freshener
a lipstick

3 What is outside the frame of each picture? (e.g. What kind of a face is this, if it is a face?) Describe the rest of the 'creature'.

4 What is the 'person' behind each of these eyes thinking about?

5 Look through the book and find another picture which could be associated with one of these eyes.

6 What piece of music would you associate with each of these eyes?

7 If you had to choose a piece of jewellery to go with each of these eyes, what would you choose? (i.e. type, size, shape, colour, type of stone, etc.)

8 Take a dictionary. Open it anywhere. Write down the first noun that you see on the right-hand page. Do this three times. You now have three nouns. Choose one of the three eyes and associate the three words with this eye in a five-line poem.

9 You have just had a dream in which one of these eyes played an important part. What was the dream about?

10.10

11 Sequences

11.1

Work in groups of three. Try to work out a coherent ordering of the pictures
opposite and find an interpretation of the story the sequence tells.
Consider the following questions:
– Where is this taking place?
– Who does the bag belong to?
– Who are the two men? Do they know each other? Do they have any official
  function?
– What does the bag contain?
– What will happen next?
Choose a secretary to write down the group's interpretation. The secretary from each
group then goes to another group to explain and defend his or her group's ordering
and interpretation.

Work in groups of three and consider the following questions:
- How many people are involved?
- Who are they?
- Is the man hammering on the door the same as the one writing the note?
- Who is the note for? Why is he writing it? What does it say?
- Why is the man hammering? What is on the other side of the door?
- What kind of place are the hands coming out of?
- Why is a hand gripping the outstretched wrist? Whose wrist is it?
- In one picture there is only one hand. Who does it belong to? What is he or she saying?

When the order and interpretation are agreed, each group should write two or three lines telling the story to accompany each picture. Each group then joins another group to exchange stories.

1 Work in groups of three or four and consider each of the drawings separately.
  Think about the following:
  – Who is the man? What sort of person is he? Easy-going? Demanding?
  – In what kind of restaurant does the scene take place?
  – What did the man order?
  Try to agree on a story to link the cartoons. When you have finished, one of you
  should go to another group and explain your version.
2 Imagine the conversation between the man and the waiter.
3 What will the man do next? Is he going to order something else? What?
4 Imagine the man ordered something else on the menu (e.g. fish, a cake). Describe a
  similar scene to fit the situation.
5 Before leaving the restaurant, the man wrote a few lines in the restaurant's book
  (where guests write down their comments). What did he write?

11.4

12 Cartoons

12.1

Work in pairs and think about the following points:
- Imagine who these two characters are. What do they do in life?
- Considering what they are thinking, can you tell anything about their respective personalities?
- Have these thoughts suddenly occurred to them? Or have they been thinking of such things for a long time? Was the picnic planned on purpose for that reason? If so, who planned it?
- Imagine how each of them spends the day.
- What led to such a situation?
- What will happen now? Will either succeed? If so, who will?
- In the drawing, the woman imagines the man's thoughts and reacts accordingly. Suppose the man can now 'see' her thoughts. What would he now think or do?
- Think of similar situations in which both the man and woman might have had similar plans.
Tell each other how you 'see' the picture.

Follow-up work

Working in pairs or in small groups, consider the following points.
1 Imagine you can, for just one minute, follow the thoughts of the man and woman. They are probably very different from what they actually say. Write down what each of them *says* during this minute, and, underneath, what each of them *thinks*.
2 One of these two characters' plans finally succeeds. Write out the short dialogue that would take place in the police station when the man or woman reports the 'accident' and is asked further questions.
3 What caption would you give this cartoon?
4 Imagine the drawing was used for an advertisement. Write out:
   - the slogan.
   - the short text (no more than five lines) that accompanied it.
5 Imagine the conversation between this couple when they were planning their picnic. Write out the most important part.

77

12.4

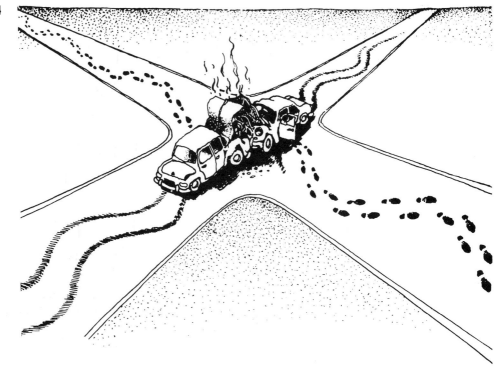

12.5

12.6

12.7

13 Split cartoons

13.1

1 Work in groups of three or four and look carefully at each of the four elements of the cartoon. First try to think of an interpretation for each element.
   – The footsteps. Whose are they?
   – The oval black object. What can it be?
   – The man with the walking-stick. What is he looking at?
   – The other man. Where is he going?
2 Decide what the relation is between the different elements. Once you have found an idea, you must also decide where each part goes in relation to the others.
3 Tell the other groups how you 'see' the picture. The other groups will try to criticise this interpretation.

Follow-up work

Work on your own first. Then compare what you've done with your partner(s).
1 The two men
   – meet.
   – collide with each other.
   Who would speak first? What would they say?
2 Suppose this cartoon – as you imagine it – appeared as an advertisement. What would it be for? What would the slogan be?

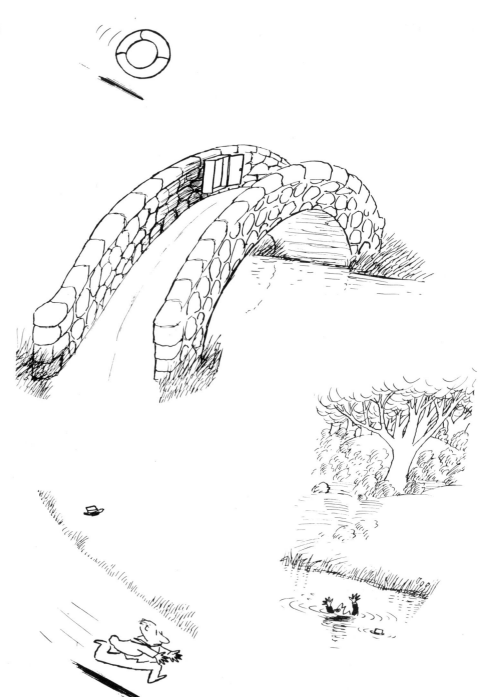

14 Minimal differences

14.1

14.2

14.3

1 Working in pairs, study all three pictures and work out the following points:
  - Are the towers in each picture the same? If not, are there two different towers, or three?
  - Are they the same people?
  - Were the pictures taken at the same time of day?
  - Was the weather the same in each?
  Change partners and compare your ideas.
2 Return to your first partner and decide what the physical surroundings are for each picture. (i.e. Where is the tower? In a village? On the coast? On top of a mountain?) Then decide who the people are, how they got there, what they are doing and what they are going to do. Be as precise as possible.
3 With a different partner, imagine that these are three scenes in a horror or suspense film. Write the part of the script that refers to this sequence. If there is no dialogue, you should describe as accurately as possible what the camera is to do (i.e. Is it fixed, hand-held, tracking in? Is a wide-angle lens being used?). Do not forget the soundtrack. What background noises are there? What music is there? Indicate what the next shot will be. Finally, give the film a title.

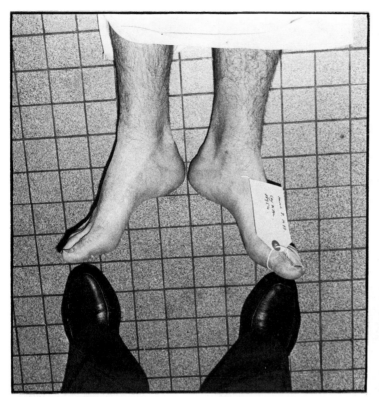

14.4

14.5

1 With a partner, look at the following series of pictures of feet. First, try to decide in each case:
   – the age and sex of the 'owner' of the feet.
   – how he or she is dressed.
   – in what position he or she is standing/sitting/lying, etc. If standing, how are the arms held? Is the person talking or not? What is he or she standing on? (The floor, probably, but *what* floor?) If the person is sitting, why is he or she sitting? Is he or she alone or in company, relaxed or tense, bored or interested?
2 Look at other pictures in the book, particularly those in sections 1 'Portraits', 3 'People', and 4 'Outside'. Choose a person to 'fit' each pair of feet, then compare your choice with that of others. Feel free to challenge any 'misfits'.

86

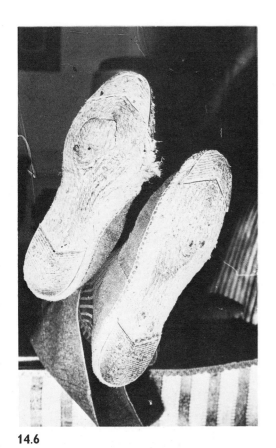

14.6

14.7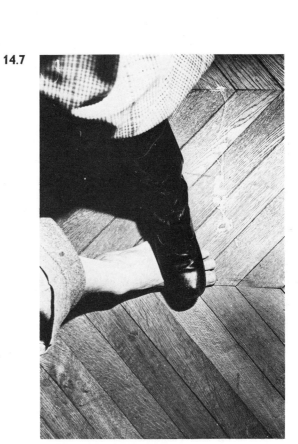

14.8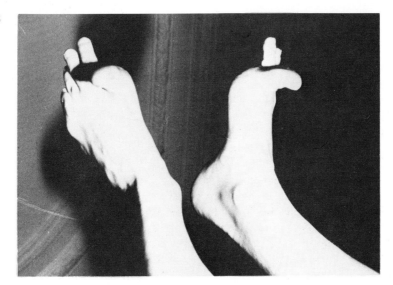

14.9

14.10

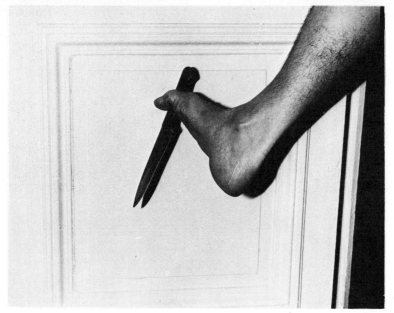

Working in pairs or in small groups look at the following series of pictures of windows and consider these points.

1. Try to imagine what kind of building each window belongs to (e.g. factory, slum, office). How high up is the window (e.g. ground floor, top floor)?
2. Try to imagine what can be seen from each of these windows (e.g. street, garden, other buildings).
3. Look at the classified advertisements for properties in an English newspaper. Then write a description of the house/flat/factory represented by each of these windows. (Remember you are trying to show it in the best possible light. Do not forget to include a price.)
4. Which of these windows would you prefer to live behind? Discuss your reasons.
5. Who do you think lives behind each of these windows? What kind of a person is he or she? Can you find a picture of a person in this book who might live behind each of these windows?
6. What do you think the room is like? Describe the furniture, type of decoration, curtains, etc.
7. These windows are all in buildings which are threatened with demolition. If you could choose two of these buildings to save, which ones would you choose?
8. Choose one of the windows. Imagine that it is important in the scenery of a play. Describe what the play is about and who the characters are.

14.11

Work in pairs. For each of the following five pictures, one person in each pair should look at one of the pictures, the other should look at the corresponding picture as shown.

Make sure that your partner cannot see your picture. Each of you takes it in turns to describe a part of the picture. Try to build up a list of the differences between your two pictures. Then finally compare your pictures.

14.13 corresponds with 1.6 (p. 11)
14.14 corresponds with 8.3 (p. 51)
14.15 corresponds with 6.5 (p. 40)
14.16 corresponds with 7.1 (p. 42)
14.17 corresponds with 10.9 (p. 66)

14.13

14.14

15 Illusions

15.1

15.2

1 Working on your own write down what you can see in each of the two pictures above.
Now work in groups of three. Discuss what you have written down. Do you agree with each other? If not, can you 'see' what your partners saw?
Discuss the interpretations as a class. How many different ideas were there?

2 *Doodles*

Write down what you think each of these pictures represents. (This can be as extraordinary and fantastic as you like.) Compare notes with a partner. Finally, in class discussion, see how many different versions there are.

15.3

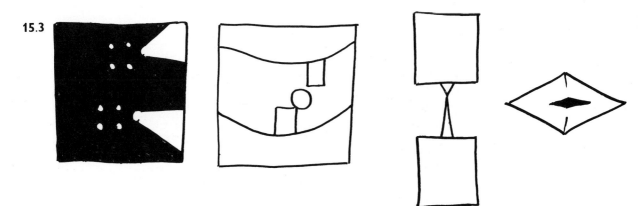

3 *Squiggles*

Work alone on the first squiggle. You can add up to five lines or dots to it to make it into a recognisable picture of something. Do not show your picture to anyone else.

Now work with a partner. Each of you should try to find out, by questioning, what the other has drawn.

With the next three squiggles work in pairs. One of you should add up to five lines or dots again, as with the first squiggle. The other should keep the squiggle as it is. Without showing what he or she has drawn, the first person should now give instructions on what lines to draw to the one with the blank squiggle. How much alike are the two drawings at the end?

15.4

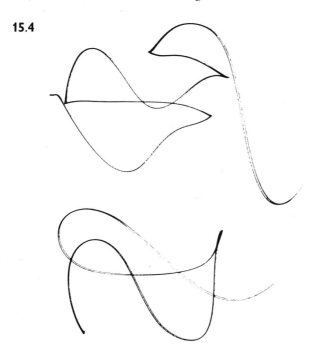